A Look at Space

The Planets

by Rebecca Sabelko

BLASTOFF! Beginners

BLASTOFF! BEGINNERS, AN IMPRINT OF BELLWETHER MEDIA BY FLUTTERBEE

Blastoff! Beginners are developed by literacy experts and educators to meet the needs of early readers. These engaging informational texts support young children as they begin reading about their world. Through simple language and high frequency words paired with crisp, colorful photos, Blastoff! Beginners launch young readers into the universe of independent reading.

Sight Words in This Book

are	in	made	red	two
four	is	of	some	up
has	it	other	the	
have	look	our	they	

This edition first published in 2027 by Bellwether Media, Inc.

For information regarding permission, write to Bellwether Media, Inc., Attention: Permissions Department, 3500 American Blvd W, Suite 150, Bloomington, MN 55431.

Library of Congress Cataloging-in-Publication Data

Names: Sabelko, Rebecca author
Title: The planets / by Rebecca Sabelko.
Description: Minneapolis, Minnesota : Bellwether Media, Inc, 2027. | Series: A look at space | Includes bibliographical references and index. | Audience: Ages 4-7 | Audience: Grades K-1 | Summary: "Developed by literacy experts and educators for students in PreK through grade two, this book introduces beginning readers to the planets through simple, predictable text and related photos"--- Provided by publisher.
Identifiers: LCCN 2026011461 (print) | LCCN 2026011462 (ebook) | ISBN 9798893049923 library binding | ISBN 9798898802776 (paperback) | ISBN 9798898801342 (ebook) Subjects: LCSH: Planets
Classification: LCC QB602 .S23 2026 (print) | LCC QB602 (ebook)
LC record available at https://lccn.loc.gov/2026011461
LC ebook record available at https://lccn.loc.gov/2026011462

ISBN: 9798893049923 (hardcover)
ISBN: 9798898802776 (paperback)
ISBN: 9798898801342 (ebook)

Editor: Suzane Nguyen Designer: Laura Sowers

Printed in the United States of America, North Mankato, MN.

Table of Contents

Mars at Night

Look up!
Mars looks red.
It is bright!

Mars

The Planets

Our **solar system** has eight planets. They are round.

solar system

They have **gravity**. It pulls things in.

ПРОГРЕСС

Four planets are made of rock.

rock

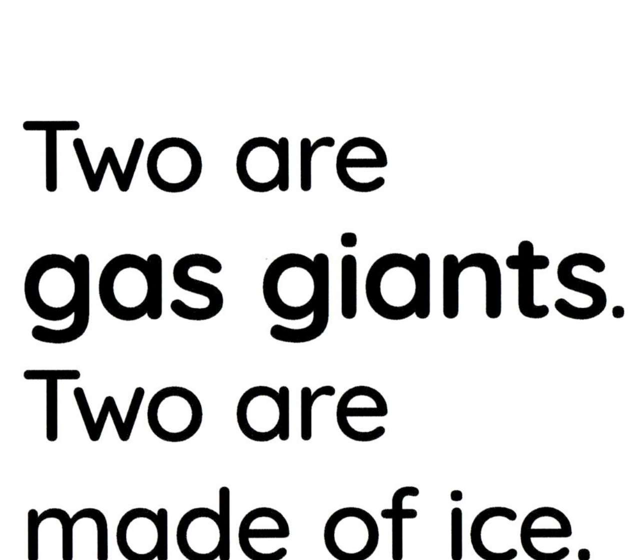

Two are **gas giants**. Two are made of ice.

ice planet

gas giant

What Planets Do

The planets move around the sun.

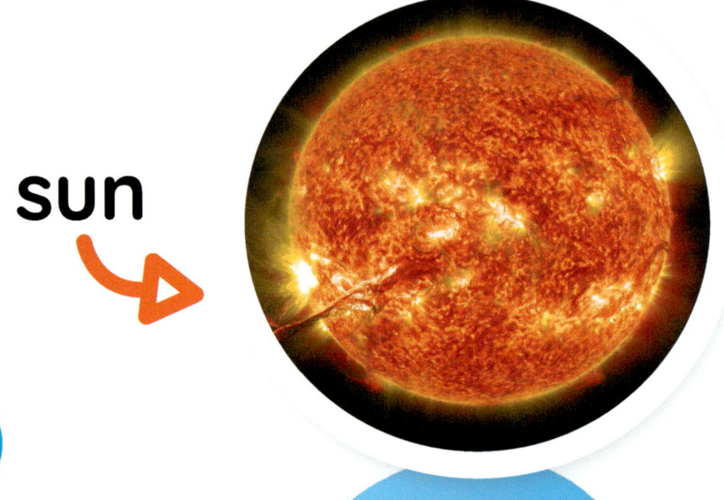

sun
planet

Some are hot.
Others are cold.

Four planets have rings. Six have moons.

moons

The planets are important parts of our solar system!

About the Planets

The Eight Planets

Things Planets Can Have

Glossary

gas giants: big planets that do not have hard places to stand on

gravity: a force that pulls objects toward each other

solar system: the sun and everything that moves around it

To Learn More

ON THE WEB

FACTSURFER

Factsurfer.com gives you a safe, fun way to find more information.

1. Go to www.factsurfer.com.
2. Enter "the planets" into the search box and click 🔍.
3. Select your book cover to see a list of related content.

Index

The images in this book are reproduced through the courtesy of: wasan, front cover, pp. 12, 22 (Uranus); MARUF Ahmed, pp. 3, 22 (Jupiter); Kevin Gill/ Wikipedia, pp. 4, 22 (Mars); Genevieve Vallee/ Alamy Stock Photo, pp. 4-5; Arina P Habich, pp. 6-7; NASA/ Flickr, pp. 8-9, 14-15; NASA/ JPL, pp. 10-11; NASA/ Wikipedia, pp. 12-13; NASA/ GSFC/ SDO/ Flickr, p. 14; NASA/ JPL/ Flickr, pp. 16-17, 18-19, 22 (gases); Trym, pp. 18, 22 (Saturn); ESO/ Y. Beletsky/ Wikipedia, pp. 20-21; SN, p. 22 (Mercury); gizemg, p. 22 (Venus); NASA Goddard Space Flight Center Image by Reto Stöckl/ Wikipedia, p. 22 (Earth); Thomas, p. 22 (Neptune); Gary, p. 22 (moons); NASA/ JPL/ USGS/ Flickr, p. 22 (rings); The Hubble Heritage Team (STScI/AURA/NASA) and Amy Simon (Cornell U.)/ Flickr, p. 23 (gas giants); wxs2102, p. 23 (gravity); PaulPaladin, p. 23 (solar system).